PRINCESS ARACOMA

PRINCESS ARACOMA:

THE SHAWNEE AND PIONEERS OF LOGAN COUNTY, WEST VIRGINIA

G.T. SWAIN

Charleston, West Virginia

Quarrier Press
Charleston, WV

Originally Published in 1927 as part of *The History of Logan County*

© 2021, Quarrier Press

All rights reserved. No part of this book may be reproduced in any form or means, electronic or mechanical, including photocopying, recording, or by any information storage and retrieval system, without permission in writing from the publisher.

Book and cover design: Mark S. Phillips
Front cover illustration: © L. Jason Queen

ISBN 13: 978-1-942294-21-4
ISBN 10: 1-942294-21-2

10 9 8 7 6 5 4 3 2 1

Printed in the United States of America

Distributed by:

West Virginia Book Co.
1125 Central Ave.
Charleston, WV 25302
www.wvbookco.com

INTRODUCTION

This book was originally part of a much larger book called History of Logan County, West Virginia; by G. T. Swain. Except for a handful of minor grammatical changes, and in spite of numerous politically incorrect instances, we have left the book as published in 1927.

Princess Aracoma was the daughter of Chief Cornstalk, the leader of the Shawnee Indians. Both Cornstalk and Aracoma are legendary and have an important place in the early history of West Virginia.

Princess Aracoma was known to be strikingly beautiful, and a fair and wise leader. Even after the unjustifiable death of her father, Aracoma led her people with dignity and strength.

Her marriage to a white man—Boling Baker, whom she dearly loved, and who treated her with every kindness and devotion, is a story told throughout West Virginia's history.

Not only does this book show the conflict and struggles between natives and settlers in the rugged land that would eventually become Logan County and surrounding areas, it conveys the gradual evolution of the land, the people, and the emergence of what would become the state of West Virginia.

Table Of Contents

Transformation of American Pioneers 1

Indian Princess Enters Guyandotte Valley 7

Battle of Point Pleasant 26

America Strikes for Liberty. 31

The White Man and the Indians Clash 42

Whites Pursue Indians In Guyan Valley 57

Battling the Indians Far In the Wilderness. 66

America Gains Her Independence. 77

Surveying Parties Enter Guyandotte Valley 82

CHAPTER I

Transformation of American Pioneers

At its outset American history discloses a novel picture of men out of an old world set upon the coasts of a new to do the work of pioneers, without suitable training either of thought or hand—men schooled in an old civilization, puzzled, even daunted, by the wilderness in which they found themselves as by a strange and alien thing, ignorant of its real character, lacking all the knowledge and craft of the primitive world, lacking everything but courage, sagacity, and a steadfast will to succeed.

As they pushed their gigantic task they were themselves transformed. The unsuitable habits of an old world fell away from them. Their old blood bred a new stock, and the youth of the race to which they belonged was renewed. And yet they did not break with the past, were for long scarcely conscious of their own transformation, held their thoughts to old channels, were frontiersmen with traditions, not of the frontier, traditions which they cherished and held very dear, of a world in which there were only ancient kingdoms and a civilization set up and perfected time out of mind.

Their muscles hardened to the work of the wilderness, they learned woodcraft and ranged the forests like men with the breeding, and quick instincts, the ready resource in time of danger of the Indian himself, and yet though upon deep problems of religion, pondered the philosophy of the universities, were partisans and followers of statesmen and parties over sea, looked to have their fashion of dress sent to them, with every other old-world trapping they could pay for by the European ships which diligently plied to their ports. Nowhere else, perhaps, is there so open and legible a record of the stiffness of thought and the flexibility of action in men, the union of youth and age, the dominion of habit reconciled with an unspoiled freshness of bold initiative.

And with the transplantation of men out of the old world into a wilderness went also the transplantation of institutions—with the same result. The new way of life and association thrust upon these men reduced the complex things of government to their simples. Within these untouched forest they resumed again, as if by an unconscious instinct, the simple organization of village communities familiar to their race long centuries before, or here and there put palisades about a group of huts meant to serve for refuge and fortress against savage enemies lurking near at hand in the coverts, and lived in their "hundreds" again under captains, to spread at last slowly into counties with familiar sheriffs and quarter-sessions.

It was as if they had brought their old-time polity with them, not in the mature root nor even in the young cutting, but in the seed merely, to renew youth and yield itself to the influences of a new soil and a new environment. It was drawn back to its essential qualities, stripped of its elaborate growth of habits, as they themselves were. All things were touched, as it were, by the light of an earlier age returned. The study of American history furnishes, as a consequence, materials such as can be found nowhere else for a discrimination between what is accidental and what is essential in English political practice. Principles developed by the long and intricate processes of the history of one country are here put to experimental test in another, where every element of life is simplified, every problem of government reduced to its fundamental formulae.

There is here the best possible point of departure, for the student who can keep his head and who knows his European history as intimately as he knows his American, for a comparative study of institutions which may some day yield us a sane philosophy of politics which shall forever put out of school the thin and sentimental theories of the disciples of Rousseau.

These are the new riches which the study of the American history is to afford in the light that now shines upon it; not national pride merely, nor merely an heroic picture of men wise beyond previous example in building States, and uniting them under a government at once free and strong, but a real understanding of the nature of liberty, of the essential character and determining circumstances of self-government, the fundamental contrasts of race and social development, of temper and of opportunity, which of themselves make governments or mar them. It may well yield us, at any rate, a few of the first principles of the natural history of institutions.

In real richness, variety, and romance, American history is full, even when we compare it with the contemporary accounts of European countries; and we know actually more of the conditions, the standards, and the social life of the American Indians in the fifteenth and sixteenth centuries than we know of the life of the English, French or German peasantry of that time.

What wonder if the early writers were a little hampered by the attempt to describe a new barbarism in terms of an old civilization? Why should not the early historian make an "emperor" out of a naked savage who had at least the physical power to sweep the Europeans off the continent if he chose? Was it not natural that "kings" and "princesses" and "noblemen" should stalk out of lodges that really held unclean and untrustworthy savages?

To Virginia, to New Amsterdam, to New England, the Indians were a mighty military power, often superior in battle, and all but victorious in the great campaign which lasted more than a hundred years. If the red man had the musket, and the white man the bow and arrow, we should to-day be writing the history of the United States "as the lion would have painted it."

In these contemporary narratives, many of them interfused with fancy and few recognizing the real squalor, degradation, and sinfulness of savage life, we have a great cycle of historical material told in the simplest historical fashion. The soul of a true son of Virginia never tires at the recital of the brave and daring deeds of the little colony which settled at Jamestown in 1607, and planted the seeds of civilization in the Western World; and the patriotic child of New England still venerates the spot where the Pilgrim Fathers landed in 1620.

With an equal veneration should we regard the hardy pioneers, who, three hundred years after the landing of Columbus, and nearly two hundred years after the planting of the colony at Jamestown, ventured into this, then, almost impenetrable wilderness, whose silence up to that time, had been unbroken, except by the roar of its clear waters as it broke over the mountain precipices, the growl of the wild beast, or the no less savage yell of the red man.

From the time of the first settlement in Virginia the aggressive spirit of the Anglo-Saxon turned his face to the wilderness of the West, and, step by step, he advanced up the James River Valley, until, reaching its head, he crossed over the mountains to the valley of the New River, where a stream running away from the sea was found.

Here the stream of civilization divided, a part of it going with the current down the Kanawha to the broad bottoms along the Ohio, and the other ascending the steeps southward towards the sources of the river, or turning a little west, to find homes among the rich coverts and verdant valleys of the Guyan River. Of such stock were the first pioneers who came here.

CHAPTER II

Indian Princess Enters Guyandotte Valley

When England assembled and transported across the broad breast of the Atlantic ocean an army of soldiers to give battle to the French and Indians on the North American continent, there was not a soldier under the command of General Braddock who stood higher in the love and esteem of his comrades than did Boling Baker.

The army fared very hard at this time and also underwent many privations. They were far from home and their loved ones, and many times the day looked dark and the spark of hope grew faint in every manly breast. Finally it began to look as if the strong would only survive the weak, as the army met disaster after disaster.

Baker was a shrewd man and possessed an intuitive brain. His willpower gave way under the continuous strain, and rather than remain with the fast dwindling troops and suffer a fate which seemed sure to overtake them, he deserted his comrades in Western Pennsylvania, on one dark night in 1756, went west into Ohio, and was taken captive by a tribe of Shawnee Indians.

The tribe of Indians took him to Chief Cornstalk, who exercised supervision over the tribe, and a council was held to determine the measure of punishment to mete out to the paleface. Very much similar to the fate of John Smith was that which met Boling Baker, for when the council of Shawnees had decided to make the white man run the gauntlet, his erect carriage and cool composure so excited the admiration of Aracoma, the young daughter of Cornstalk, that she persuaded her kindly old father to spare his life and permit him to become a member of the tribe.

Tradition has it that Aracoma at this time was a maiden of about sixteen summers in whose face was the bloom of youth, and whose countenance was good to look upon. Grateful to his benefactress and desiring to express his gratitude, Baker used every known method in his artful calendar to win her favor and make himself understood.

His chance meetings became more frequent, and meantime the little god of love was doing his shy work. Boling Baker became madly infatuated with the Indian maiden and paid her ardent court.

Meantime, the tribe had migrated to the eastern side of the Ohio River and pitched their wigwams on soil which lies near Point Pleasant, at the mouth of the Kanawha Valley.

During this time Aracoma grew in beauty and grace. She was approaching the day when she would be given authority over a part of the tribe and would bear the proud distinction of ruling as a Princess. Nature was kind to her, and the outdoor life, the soft summer zephyrs, together with an abundance of athletic exercise, tended to bring out all the latent qualities which mounted a ruddy glow to her soft copper complexion and to her cheeks the russet of health and youth. Not only had she grown in beauty, but nature had molded her after the pattern of the goddess Venus. Due to her habits of life, she had rounded into physical perfection, was lithe in body and walked with stately grace.

Perhaps Aracoma did not have the advantages of the many artificial substitutes now found at all drug stores, nor did she know of the many cosmetics. However, it is known that there were many kinds of paint used by Indians in those days and while Aracoma, due to her official position, probably used these sparingly, it was not at all necessary, for nature had done her work well and with precision.

Aracoma came into possession of her crown, was designated Princess, and given a tribe of her race over which to exercise supervision before she even accepted the affections of Baker. Well knowing that it would be necessary for her to take her subjects to new pastures, she dispatched her faithful scouts into the wilderness to search out a future place of abode.

After many moons had passed, and the scouts had covered mile after mile of valley and crossed many mountain ranges they returned, footsore and weary, with the happy news that the land of promise had been found.

Meantime, Baker had won the favor of the tribe and, due to his attentions to their Princess, whose every wish was instantly gratified by him, he was looked upon with awe and admiration. He was good to the tribe and his worldly knowledge stood him in good stead. During the time of the preparation for the long march, and waiting for the time when physical recuperation of their faithful scouts would permit their departure, he laid siege to Aracoma's heart, and finally the wall surrounding the affections of this tribal Princess capitulated and she accepted him.

The day of departure drew near and on the evening previous to their departure, when all the chiefs of the nearby tribes had arrived to pay their fond farewell, the Indian Princess arose and in true Indian fashion made known to the members of her race, there assembled, that upon arrival at their new place of abode, three moons later, she would become the wife of a paleface.

Strange to say, her announcement proved instantly pleasing. Aracoma was held in high esteem by all of her people; and the very announcement of any step that would bring her happiness was gratifying to the assembled tribes. Baker was idolized that night and the early part of the night witnessed an Indian celebration never before exceeded in tribal assemblies.

They only ceased in order to permit a few hours of rest before the sturdy band, under their new ruler, would break asunder the ties of friendship and affection, and follow her into new lands, to serve her and make for themselves new places of abode.

The day broke fair and warm on a spring day in April 1765, when the noble band was led up the Kanawha Valley and marched along the banks of that majestic river. The scouts were far in the lead and the courageous band following were strung out for many miles. It consisted of a few old Indians, and some of tender years, but the majority were sturdy bucks with their squaws who shouldered the burdens lightly.

Aracoma was in the midst of them, steadfastly attended by Baker, while the expert hunters of the tribe, with their bows and arrows, circled the band on all sides in quest of game on which they must subsist during the days of their march.

Tradition does not record the number of days during which they marched, but they left the Kanawha somewhere near the present site of St. Albans and came up the Coal River. Every night witnessed many campfires around which the tribe would gather while the faithful squaws would prepare the evening meal. The Ruler of the Universe was kind to them, for He blessed them with fair weather. The forests furnished them with food and the babbling mountain streams quenched their thirst.

Reaching the top of the mountain range, which is now the famous Blair Mountain, they were informed by their guides that they were drawing near to their new hunting grounds. Hearts were made happy and burdens lightened as they quickened their steps and marched down the mountainside—coming down what is now Dingess Run to what promised to be to them a land of milk and honey.

During the time of the entire march, the fact that their Princess was betrothed and that the union would be consummated on arrival in the land of promise was never for a moment forgotten. The entire march was attended with the beating of tom-toms, which, with the weird Indian yells, reverberated from the dense forests and echoed from the mountainside.

Perhaps no crowned head ever entered a new kingdom surrounded with more pomp and ceremony than did Aracoma. Her subjects were loyal and devoted and worshiped at her feet. During all the ceremony attending her entrance into a dense, unknown wilderness, Aracoma held herself in stately grace with modesty becoming her position. She ruled with a compassionate hand.

The evening sun was sinking behind the western hills, the mantle of darkness was covering the valleys, and their hazy borders were creeping to the mountain crests when the tribe finally reached the banks of the placid Guyan, crossed half of the stream and cast their burdens on the soil of the island just opposite Logan's present railway passenger station.

Camp fires were hastily built, the day's game was brought in, a few fish were hooked from the lazily flowing stream and after the evening repast was over the tribe cast themselves down on the verdant soil to rest their weary bodies from days of marching and labor.

The first rays of light were just stretching their fingers over the eastern horizon when the tribal band arose and hastily prepared for their morning meal. The repast was soon consumed and the loyal band then engaged in a day of bustle and activity, as all hands prepared the tepees and wigwams, and each member selected for himself a suitable place for his future abode. True to Indian fashion, the lodges were built in a circle and the largest was appropriately dedicated to Aracoma, their comely ruler.

The ground was cleared away, the wigwams built, canoes were constructed from the bark of the trees, while the fishermen of the tribe journeyed to the stream and engaged in their favorite, but necessary, pastime. The hunters were sent out and explored their new surroundings. Fish and game were found in abundance.

In season the mountain soil brought forth the blackberry and services, and the emigrant tribe literally believed they had found "the land of milk and honey."

Indian scouts were sent out to explore the country and sentinels were posted on the high mountain peaks, for it was not yet known how near their new-found home might border upon the settlements of the whites, their much-hated enemies.

After a few days these same scouts returned with information that they had journeyed miles around the camp but had failed to find any trace of the white man and that the whole country abounded in fish and game. Thus the tribe settled down in peace and quiet to begin new associations, but not forgetting broken ties nor friends left behind. Hope loomed high for a wonderful crop of Indian maize as they stirred the rich, soft soil for the annual planting.

Thus was happiness established in the new Indian village on the banks of the Guyan. Runners were dispatched to notify members of the race left behind on the banks of the beautiful Ohio, that several moons had passed and the wedding day was now near at hand.

Great preparations were made for the event. The choicest venison was prepared from the young deer that fell at the unerring aim of the hunters of the tribe. Fish were hooked from the streams while the mountains gave forth their choicest viands for the memorable event. Everything was in readiness when the chiefs and rulers, in great numbers, arrived to witness the ceremony.

The celebration lasted for three days amid the incessant beating of the tom-toms, the fantastic dances of the chiefs and squaws, and the loud ringing cry of the savages, as they bellowed forth their Indian calls. Salutations mounted high and rang from the surrounding cliffs, and re-echoed from the mountainsides.

When night came on and the stars peeked out from their mantle of deepest blue, huge bonfires were built on the high pinnacles which cast weird shadows across the valley below and played fantastic tricks amid the shadows that hung over the little island in the river below.

The actual wedding ceremony was scheduled for the second evening and just after dusk had hovered over the valley a full moon peeked above the horizon and cast soft rays of mellow light on the scene below, while the kindly old face incased therein, seemed to smile in pleasure. Aracoma emerged from her wigwam wearing the choicest of Indian robes that had been furnished by the beasts of the forest, and ornaments of brightest hue.

Baker met her with the best Indian raiment that he had been able to procure, and while a large circle was formed Chief Cornstalk, the father of the bride, stepped forward and performed the Indian rites in most approved tribal fashion and melodramatic manner.

Just as the savage ritual was completed, Aracoma

turned to her newly made husband. With shapely, soft arms outstretched, she reached up, circling them about his neck while he embraced her and drew her close to his bosom. Her lips were upturned and when they met those of her lover and chosen life companion the fire of love and devotion which had kindled and nurtured her in her heart overran its confines.

Her whole soul was flooded with waves of joy and ecstasy as she pledged to him her undying love and devotion amid the kisses showered upon her by a paleface born in foreign fields, who had ridden the rolling waves, but by Fate had been thrown into her company and now loyally and faithfully returned her every affection.

Quiet reigned on the fourth morning and the visiting members of the tribes took their departure after leaving at the door of the newly wedded couple all the various and numerous articles they had brought from a distance to present on this happy occasion.

The tribe prospered and lived a life of ease. Game was plentiful and easily obtained. All was well in camp until a year following when a new arrival made its appearance in camp. Aracoma had given birth to a baby boy. It is a long-standing custom of the Indians to name their new babies after the first object viewed by the mother following the birth of the child. Aracoma, gazing from the front of her tepee, looked out upon the rippling waters of the Guyan, and christened the new son Waulalisippi, which translated, means "Laughing Waters."

The Indian village was highly excited over the new arrival while the squaws made haste to select their prettiest beads, which they carried as a present to the newborn babe. The hunters departed into the forests and returned with choice furs which they laid at his feet, and very few babies came into this world with more adulation than did "Laughing Waters," the first born of Aracoma.

During the years that followed, other babies came to grace the home. The second was a girl and was christened "Snow Lily" when translated. The next was a girl and she bore the name of "Princess Raindrop." The fourth was a boy to be called "Running Deer," to be followed by another boy who was given the name of "Little Black Bear." The sixth and last child born to Aracoma was a girl and she was christened "Blue Feather."

The years passed by and in the year of 1776 a great scourge came upon the little Indian village. One by one the inhabitants fell sick. The medicine men, far and wide, were sent for and came — but of no avail. They were powerless to stave off the evil spirit which they thought had fallen upon the village and a large number were taken away by the hand of death. During the siege all the six little ones of Aracoma passed away and they, with the other dead of the tribe, were brought across the river and buried in the bottom with their faces to the setting sun.

After days of convalescence, while the surviving members were regaining their health and strength, the little model Indian village was sadly neglected. The food was scarce and suffering prevailed where there had previously been peace and plenty. The ensuing days were hard on the survivors. They had lost their morale and the great plague had left them with little hope.

Perhaps they would have drifted back to their old haunts, but Baker went among them and bade them to be of good cheer, for a better day was breaking. During all this time Baker proved a devoted husband to the Indian Princess. They were a happy and contented couple and there were none who found more comfort and consolation in one another's presence.

The years grew harder and each witnessed returning sickness. The savage tribe firmly believed they were cursed and were all but ready to give up their home and return to the banks of the Ohio, when Baker conceived a plan of wandering east until he came in contact with the settlements of the whites whom they knew were in that direction.

Accordingly, in the spring of 1780, a stranger appeared in the settlements of Bluestone River with woe-begone countenance and recited sorrowful accounts of the hardships he had undergone as a captive among the Indians of Ohio. He excited the pity of the settlers and they took him in without any suspicion. For a month he went from place to place among them, acquainting himself with the surroundings.

One morning, about the middle of April, when the pioneers went to the stables to feed their horses for the day's plowing, every stable was found empty. The farmers reported their loss to John Breckenridge, a young man at the next settlement, who held the position of deputy sheriff under Sheriff William Ingles, of Montgomery County. Breckenridge, in turn, notified Sheriff Ingles at the county seat of Montgomery, and in the meantime, while awaiting word from his superior, began to make preparations for a pursuit of the Indians.

Sheriff Ingles arrived at the settlement to find everything in readiness for a hasty pursuit and after a consultation held that night it was decided that Sheriff Ingles would not accompany the party, but he arranged to send ninety men under the command of General William Madison and John Breckenridge to recover the horses.

The young men of the party were eager to start on the journey and they sat up that night discussing the manner of pursuit, but at dawn the following morning heavy clouds had gathered and it began to rain. Nothing daunted, the noble, brave band bade adieu to loved ones and pushed forward on their journey.

After they reached the crest of the mountains the clouds began to drift away and through the rift the sun began to cast its early morning rays, gladdening the hearts of the brave band and enabling them to make better progress.

They followed the trail from Bluestone to Tug River, across Gilbert Creek, down it to the mouth of Horsepen Fork. Madison and his men, instead of following the trail up the Horsepen, came down Gilbert to the Guyan River and down the river to the mouth of Dingess Run.

They went into camp on the upper side of Dingess Run and two alert and experienced scouts were sent out to search for Indian signs. The two scouts who went down the river were gone for some time but upon their return they reported that about two miles west of their camp a creek came in from the west side of the river; that at the mouth of the creek there was an island situated in the center of the river which was covered with cane, and among this cane they observed a number of Indian lodges; that horses were grazing and braves were lounging around the lodges.

Madison was convinced by this report that these were the Indians he was trailing, and the next morning he dispatched scouts to the top of the mountain back of Logan to look down on the island and ascertain their number. The morning proved to be a misty one and a heavy fog hung over the river like a pall. The scouts were unable to obtain the desired information.

After the scouts returned a council of war was held and it was decided to send forty-five men, under John

Breckenridge, across the river to remain hidden until after dark, when they were to proceed down the east bank of the river, cross Island Creek, and attack the Indians.

In the meantime Madison was to take the other forty-five men down the river to where the Chesapeake & Ohio Railway "Y" was at one time situated, to be ready to receive the Indians when they started to retreat from the island. In the afternoon, Breckenridge saw from his position on the hill above Island Creek that the Indians had discovered that enemies were near. They were running wildly about, getting ready to fight, and crossing the river in their canoes. He dispatched a messenger to General Madison with this information and Madison hurried his men down the river to surprise and intercept the Indians.

They met in the bottom where Logan now stands and the fighting immediately began. The fight lasted for three hours, ten or twelve Indians were killed, several wounded, and the wounded put to death, for at that time nobody wanted to be bothered with a wounded Indian. Fifty horses, fifty bushels of corn and a few cows were captured and ten Indian lodges were burned.

Among the wounded Indians was one whose dress and actions indicated she had considerable authority and influence over the others. She was reticent at first and refused to talk. Madison used every method in his power to learn something of her history and of the tribe over which she evidently presided, but with the stoicism of her race she refused to talk.

Then, when the outstretched wings of the death angel came hovering near, she opened her eyes, gazed far beyond earth's horizon, looked up into the vast expanse of God's blue canopy, and far across the Great Divide she could see members of her race who had gone before, trooping, trooping, trooping onward to the happy hunting ground.

At last, seeming to become conscious of the fact that there was no hope of ever being recaptured by her people, she called for General Madison and thus addressed him in broken English:

> *My name is Aracoma (meaning a corn blossom) and I am the last of a mighty line. My father was a great chief and a friend of your people. He was murdered in cold blood by your people when he had come to them as a friend to give them warning. I am the wife of a paleface who came across the great waters to make war on my people, but came to us and was made one of us.*
>
> *A great plague many moons ago carried off my children with a great number of my people and they lie buried just above the bend of the river. Bury me with them with my face toward the setting sun that I may see my people in their march to the happy hunting grounds. For your kindness I warn you to make haste in returning to your*

homes, for my people are still powerful and will return to avenge my death.

Before morning dawned her proud spirit had taken its eternal flight. The next day the white men buried Aracoma, the daughter of Cornstalk, in the lot above mentioned.

Having accomplished the purpose of the expedition, General Madison and his men turned their faces homeward and began their weary march across the mountains to their friends and loved ones left behind.

During the battle Boling Baker was absent. He had gone far back into the mountains hunting for wild game for food for the colony. He made haste to return and reached the crest of the mountain west of the island just as the battle was over. Realizing that his people had all been annihilated, he sat down on a stone and wept as a child for many hours.

With bleeding heart and heavy tread he turned his face westward and wandered off. Where he went was never ascertained, but many years later an aged man came wandering up the Guyan River, inquiring of the white settlers who had then moved in, certain facts. It is said he stood for many hours on the mountain side weeping, then wended his way onward up the stream, and a day later was found dead in bed near what is now Man, where he had been given lodging by a kindly settler.

As the pioneer settlers reached the crest of the

mountains on their return they signaled to their loved ones in the valleys below by the firing of many guns. The signal was passed on from farm settlement to every mountain cabin, and as the returning troops came marching in they were received with wild excitement not unmixed with anxiety as to the number who failed to return. It was ascertained that all had returned and none of them had suffered injury.

The mountain cabins rang that night with the sound of the fiddle and banjo, and the maidens of the settlement were happily swung about by the sturdy members as they danced the Old Virginia reel.

The participants were hailed as heroes and were kept busy for days later telling of the incidents of the journey and of the battle far in the heart of the vast wilderness.

The story has been told and retold in every household on the old time frontier and has been handed down from generation to generation. From the retelling of this story in its original form the fragments of this narrative have been obtained and here compiled for the glorification and to the sacred memory of Aracoma, an Indian princess, who never knew civilization, but who loved her people and who ruled over them with tenderness and compassion.

Like unto her father she was not aggressive, nor did she store within her heart hatred for the white man. For her sacred marriage to a paleface, whom she dearly loved, and who treated her with every kindness and devotion, she was willing to die and forgive, even though it was through his instrumentality that she must suffer death.

CHAPTER III

Battle Of Point Pleasant

The Battle of Point Pleasant, fought on the 10th day of October, 1774, between the mountaineers of Virginia, under the command of General Andrew Lewis, upon the one side, and the confederated Indian tribes, under the command of Cornstalk, the great Sachem of the Shawnees, on the other, is justly considered by many as the first battle of the Revolution.

Before the Virginians left their homes, the spirit of independence was fast asserting itself in the counties beyond the Blue Ridge. Thomas Jefferson, Patrick Henry, Peyton Randolph, Richard Henry Lee, and a host of others were asserting the rights of British freemen, and denouncing the oppressive act of Parliament. The first Continental Congress was in session at Philadelphia, with Peyton Randolph, of Virginia, as its President, and Patrick Henry, George Washington, Richard Bland, Benjamin Harrison and Edmund Pendleton were the other members from Virginia.

Twice had Governor Dunmore dissolved the Virginia Assembly because it had dared to express its sympathy with the people of Boston in their struggle for commercial freedom, and now this same Governor, with the forces which he had gathered in the northern part of the colony, had broken faith with General Lewis by failing to keep his appointment with him, leaving his little force to meet the onslaught of the braves under Cornstalk, while he (Governor Dunmore) was trying to effect a treaty with all the Indian tribes. What this treaty was the Virginians under General Lewis could only guess, but subsequent events proved only too clear its object.

After the battle of Point Pleasant, General Lewis marched with the major part of his command eighty miles across the Ohio wilderness to Congo Creek, when he was ordered by Governor Dunmore to halt, although he was in striking distance of the Indian towns, and his men ready for the fray.

A portion of Lewis' command was left at Point Pleasant where they hastily erected a fort, which, in honor of the first President of the Continental Congress, they named Fort Randolph.

A few days afterward the treaty of peace was effected, and, by order of Governor Dunmore, a junction of the two divisions was formed and the whole army returned to Virginia by way of Fort Gower, at the mouth of the Muskingum. It was at this old fort on the

5th day of November, 1774, that the Virginians forming the two divisions met to take counsel with each other as to their duty in the impending struggle between the patriots and the royalists in the East.

In this meeting resolutions were adopted assuring their brethren of the East that their service under Governor Dunmore must not be construed as acquiescence in the recent acts of Parliament, but that it had been for the protection of their homes and the people of Virginia. They boldly declared their attachment to the cause of independence, and their zeal for the honor and liberty of all the American colonies.

One of the resolutions is as follows; "As attachment to the real interests and just rights of American outweigh every other consideration, we resolve that we will exert every power within us for the defense of American liberty, when regularly called for by the unanimous voice of our countrymen."

These proceedings were not such as Governor Dunmore had hoped for. His deputy, Dr. Connelly, of Pennsylvania, who had declared himself the magistrate of West Augusta, was the cause of the hostility between the whites and Indians, yet was unrebuked by the Governor.

It was well known to him that a trader by the name of Greathouse was the murderer of the family of Logan, the Cayuga Chief, and yet, in order to incite the Indians against the Americans, the murder was laid upon

Captain Cresap, a brave soldier and pioneer.

Captain Cresap did what he could to prevent the outbreak, and was at the time of the murder with his family in Maryland. He thought, doubtless, that when he left Williamsburg, by his prompt action in marching to the frontier, he would be able to attach the mountaineers to the royal cause, or, failing in this, that he would place such enmity between the whites and Indians as to make it impossible for the whites of the frontier to give any assistance to their brethren in the East, and that they would be kept busy protecting their homes from the torch, and their wives and children from the tomahawk and scalping-knife of the savage, while English soldiers would crush the spirit of liberty out of the rebels.

However, he was doomed to disappointment. The pioneers were truly American, and as such, were in full sympathy with the cause of liberty, and the brave fight made by Lewis' eleven hundred broke the backbone of the Indian confederacy.

Leaving Fort Gower on the morning of November 6th, the northern division, under Governor Dunmore, took the usual route to the headwaters of the Potomac, while the southern division, under Lewis, turned down the Ohio to Point Pleasant, and leaving a portion of the command at Fort Randolph for the protection of the frontier, returned to their homes by the new route of Kanawha Valley.

The election for members of Parliament in England, which had taken place in October, 1774, so strengthened King George and his ministry that when petitions for the redress of the grievous wrongs which had been perpetrated upon New England colonies were presented to the King, he haughtily replied: "The New England governments are now in a state of rebellion. Blows must decide whether they are to be subject to this country, or are to be independent."

This ultimatum of the King was promptly met by the American colonies with a determination to free themselves from the unjust exactions of the Crown and his Parliament. Determined not to strike the first blow, they buckled on their armor and waited for the attack.

CHAPTER IV

America Strikes For Liberty

On the 19th day of April 1775, just as the sun was lifting itself from the bosom of the Atlantic to diffuse its light and warmth over the hills of New England, the rattle of musketry broke the stillness of the air on the Lexington commons, which, being heard by Samuel Adams, caused him to exclaim, "What a glorious morning for America is this!"

American blood was shed because freemen had refused to disperse at the command of a British major. On the next day—April 20th—Governor Dunmore, maddened by his experience in the West and the bold declarations of the people east of the Blue Ridge, as well as in obedience to an order from the British Government, secretly removed all the gunpowder belonging to the colony from Williamsburg to a British man-of-war lying at anchor at Yorktown, and offered freedom to all negro slaves belonging to rebels who would enlist under the British flag.

The news of the battle of Lexington and of the high-handed measures of Governor Dunmore reach the bold yeomanry of Fincastle at the same time, and as the news spread from settlement to settlement in the upper valley of the Roanoke, and New and the Clinch, the plow stood still in the furrow, and the planting of the crop, which was then in progress, was suspended, as earnest and determined men met in groups to discuss the situation and determine upon their line of duty.

To them the situation was not a pleasant one. To the west was a vast wilderness inhabited by a wily and savage race who knew every pass in the mountains, and were able to swoop down upon the unprotected homes without warning. East of them were their fathers and brothers engaged in a struggle for liberty, while Governor Dunmore was trying to incite a servile insurrection by urging the negro to deeds of murder and rapine under the protection of the British flag.

They had an equal desire for, and interest in liberty and independence as the people of the East, and at once decided that while a portion of them would remain to protect their homes against the savage, others would hold themselves in readiness to go wherever Virginia might call fully, endorsing the resolution that was adopted by the citizen-soldiery, which met at Fredericksburg on the 25th day of April, 1775, that they would "defend by force of arms this or any sister colony from unjust or wicked invasion."

On the 30th of June 1775, the Virginia Assembly declared that Governor Dunmore had abdicated his office, and called a convention to meet at Richmond on the 17th day of July, for the purpose of organizing a government for the colony, and of agreeing upon a plan of defense. This convention appointed a Committee of Safety and called for 9,000 volunteers.

Before the frosts of autumn had prepared the grain for harvest, two hundred men from the District of Fincastle had taken up their line of march for the valley to enlist under the banner which had inscribed upon its folds, "VIRGINIA FOR CONSTITUTIONAL LIBERTY," and which had been placed in the hands of Colonel John Peter Gabriel Muhlenberg, the patriotic preacher at Woodstock, who, taking as his text, "There is a time for all things: a time to preach and a time for fight, and now is the time to fight," from which he preached a patriotic sermon, and then, marching down from the pulpit, read his commission as colonel of the Virginia forces and commenced enlisting men for his regiment.

Among the brave yeomanry going out from Fincastle to join Muhlenberg we find the names of Adams, Altizer, Ballard, Baillard, Bailey, Baker, Brown, Browning, Buchanan, Burgess, Chafin, Chapman, Chambers, Clark, Cline, Conley, Cook, Davis, Dempsey, Dingess, Doss, Ellis, Farley, Ferrell, Finch, Fry, Garrett, Godby, Gore, Henderson, Hill, Hatfield,

Jackson, Justice, Johnson, McDonald, Mc- Neely, Mullins, Meade, Musick, McCoy, Morgan, Perry, Runyon, Scaggs, Smith, Stafford, Stone, Stollings, Taylor, Toler, Vance, Varney, White, and many others whose names are familiar in every neighborhood of Logan County who were the sires of the brave men who conquered our wilderness and established a community noted for bravery, hospitality and patriotism.

The tale of how, through suffering, privation and danger, they, with their comrades of all the Thirteen Colonies, discharged their duty until the final victory at Yorktown, has been told so often in song and story that the world knows it by heart.

The deeds of daring against the frequent and barbarous raids of the Indians, are not less glorious than are those of the men who went to the front, but they are not known to the world; they live alone in tradition and in the memory of a generation which is fast fading away.

It is not the soil or climate, the lofty mountain peaks, the broad, fertile valleys, the wealth or timber that makes a country. It is rather the character of its people. The character of the first settlers of a country makes a lasting impression, and one that cannot be effaced by subsequent immigration. It is due to this fact that we find Virginia and Massachusetts, today, English in all of their characteristics. It was the Englishman—the Cavalier and the Puritan—that first planted civilization in these colonies and shaped the development of their affairs.

About the year of 1732 the lower valley around Winchester was settled with Germans and Scotch-Irish from Pennsylvania, and from them the settlements were made in West Augusta. Fincastle, however, was settled by the sons of the planters and small landowners from the valley of the James, and by the sons of the men of Ulster, who came over with the Huguenot, John Lewis, in 1737, to escape the religious persecutions in England.

All of them were distinctively Virginian. Born and reared upon its soil they knew no other country, and while they were loyal to the King and his Lord Lieutenant, yet their first allegiance to the State which their fathers had erected in the American wilderness. Class distinction was broken down and the honest pioneer was not asked whether he was the son of a rich planter, the small landowner or the late emigrant from Ulster.

The religious persecutions of the lowlands were unknown, and Catholics, Episcopalians, Presbyterians, Baptists, and Quakers were allowed to worship God in their own way. Class and religious distinctions having been in this way obliterated, they were ready when the time came to strike as one man for liberty.

Noble men were these sires of ours; setting their feet firmly upon the outpost of civilization, their eyes were turned toward the setting sun, with the determination to possess the country and conquer the wilderness, though every step in that direction was contested by a savage foe. Yet, amid it all, they kept their ears open to the cry of the patriots in the lowlands, and held themselves in readiness to buckle on their armor in defense of Virginia and her sister colonies.

With the people of Virginia the right of self-government in local affairs, which had first been granted to them by James I, was held to be sacred, and was retained by them in the surrender made to Cromwell, and was regranted or continued to them when Charles II was restored to the throne.

This second Magna Carta was carried in the bosoms of these young Virginians to their mountain homes. So we find that while West Augusta was contented to be ruled by Governor Dunmore's Lieutenant, Dr. John Connelly, Fincastle, in 1772 demanded local self-government and the appointment of officers who resided within the District, and while the rights of a county were not conceded, the Governor was compelled to grant the request of naming it a county, and appointing justices, a sheriff and a clerk who resided within it bounds, and making it entirely independent of the county of Botetourt, yet including within its boundary all of Southwestern Virginia, and the present State of Kentucky.

The following officers were appointed for the new county thus established: Gentlemen Justices,

William Ingles, Robert Doach, Jas McGavock, Stephen Trigg, Walter Crockett, James Thompson and Arthur Campbell; Sheriff, William Preston; Clerk, John Byrd, who admitted Colonel William Christian as his Deputy. This first court for the County of District was held on the 5th day of January, 1773. No representative, however, was allowed them in the House of Burgesses.

By the ordinance of the Virginia Convention which convened at Richmond on the 17th day of July, 1775, providing for the election of delegates to the convention which was called to meet at Williamsburg on the 6th day of May, 1776, the right of franchise was granted to the inhabitants of Fincastle and West Augusta, and Colonel William Christian was elected from Fincastle as a member of the convention and participated with all the members of the convention in the following resolution:

"That the delegates appointed to represent this colony in general Congress be instructed to propose to that respectable body to declare the United Colonies free and independent States, absolved from all allegiance to, or dependence on the Crown or Parliament of Great Britain; and that they give the assent of this Colony to such declaration, and whatever measures may be thought necessary by Congress for forming foreign alliances and a confederation of colonies at such time and in the manner that to them shall seem best; provided that the power of forming governments for, and the regulations of the internal concerns of each colony, be left to the colonial legislature."

On the 27th day of June of the same year, the convention adopted by a unanimous vote a constitution in which the ties, which bound it to Great Britain, were entirely dissolved, and Virginia declared a free and independent State.

At the meeting of the Legislature after the adjournment of the convention, the County of District of Fincastle was divided, the present counties of Washington, Russel, Smythe, Buchanan, Dickinson, Lee, Scott and Wise, and portions of the present counties of Grayson, Tazewell and Wythe becoming the county of Washington, and portions of the present counties of Grayson, Tazewell and Wythe and the whole of the present counties of Carroll, Bland, Floyd, Montgomery, Giles and Craig of Virginia, and Greenbrier, Monroe, Mercer, Summers, Fayette, Kanawha, Mason, Putnam, McDowell, Raleigh, Wyoming, Logan, Mingo, Lincoln, Cabell, Boone and Wayne, of West Virginia, were established as a county, and in honor of the brave Irish general, who, with his blood, sealed his devotion to the cause of American liberty before the redoubts of Quebec, was called Montgomery, and Fincastle ceased to exist as a county or district of Virginia.

Of the first court for Kentucky, Colonel John Floyd, father of John Floyd, afterwards Governor of Virginia, and grandfather of our late venerable countryman, Colonel G. R. C. Floyd, and who had resided with and was deputy surveyor under Colonel Preston of Montgomery, was a member.

The first court of Washington was held at Abingdon, and among its justices were John Campbell, father of David Campbell who was afterwards Governor of Virginia. His brother, Robert Campbell, was also a member of the court, and his brother, David Campbell, was the first clerk.

The first court of Montgomery County was held at old Fort Chiswell—now in Wythe County—on the 7th day of January, 1777. Colonel William Preston, John Montgomery, Stephen Trigg, Jas McGavock and James McCorkle were the justices who organized the court. William Ingles was appointed sheriff, and John Byrd was appointed clerk, with William Littlepage as his deputy.

Colonel William Preston was one of the best-known men of his day. As surveyor of Botetourt County, residing in the district of Fincastle, he had done nearly all of the surveying in the district and was personally acquainted with nearly every family in it.

He was quite wealthy and in addition to fitting out several companies from Montgomery County to do service with Colonels William and John Campbell in the Carolinas, he, together with Dr. Thomas Walker and Edmund Pendleton, fitted out a privateer and placed it under the command of Colonel John Floyd, above mentioned.

He also had a son, James Patton Preston, and two grandsons, John B. Floyd and James McDowell, who were afterwards Governors of Virginia. It is a little remarkable that each of the Presidents of the County Courts appointed by Patrick Henry for the first three counties created by the State of Virginia and carved out of the old district of Fincastle should raise a son who should be Governor of the State.

Colonel William Preston was also a member of the first Legislature of the State, as the colleague to Colonel William Christian, who had been mentioned as the commander of the Fincastle troops at Point Pleasant, and as a member of the Virginia Convention. Colonel Christian was one of the most influential members of that first State Legislature. He was not so well versed in books or so eloquent as many of his associates, but he was in close touch with the people, and, fully understanding their wishes, he had the courage to represent them.

In addition to the soldiers heretofore mentioned, Montgomery raised a battalion of artillery which was placed under the command of Major John Trigg, and more than half of Colonel Abraham Trigg's infantry regiment, both of which commands were under the command of La Fayette, and participated in the siege of Yorktown, while one company of the glorious band which, under the leadership of George Rogers Clark, the Hannibal of the West, saved the Northwest territory to Virginia, was from Montgomery County.

Colonel William Ingles also kept in the country, as a guard against Indian depredations, a picked body of men, among who were some of the finest Indian scouts of the day, some of who will hereafter be mentioned. Immigration instead of being checked by the war, increased, and from 1775 to 1782, the population had more than doubled, and many settlements had been made within the limits of the present State of West Virginia.

CHAPTER V

The White Man And The Indians Clash

After the battle of Point Pleasant most of the regular Indian Settlements on the Virginia side of the Ohio River were broken up and, except for the purposes of hunting, the whole country was abandoned.

Evidences of settlement are found in different parts of the county, both in Guyandotte and Sandy Valleys. At several places in both valleys there are at present large mounds, which show that the mound builders had possessed the country at one time. Who were these people? What was their occupation? These are questions that so far have failed of an answer. That they were here there can be no doubt.

The carved stones, inscriptions, copper plates of unique design, and ornaments of mica and shells are not the work of the Indians whose manufacturing industries were confined to the making of canoes from bark or skins, garments of skin, and weapons and agricultural implements of stone.

In 1777 an alliance was formed between the British Government and all of the Indian tribes north of the Ohio, with the exception of the Shawnees, who were disposed to be friendly with the Americans, and in the summer of that year. Cornstalk, the great Sachem of the Shawnees, came to Fort Randolph in order to apprise the garrison, and at the same time to show his friendship for the men who had defeated him at that place as well as to show them that on account of the treaty made between England and the other tribes, the Shawnees would be driven to take sides with the enemy.

In order to prevent this, Cornstalk was detained at the fort. During his stay two of the garrison crossed the Ohio River for the purpose of hunting and one of them was killed. This so inflamed the passions of the men at the fort that Cornstalk, his son and another Indian chief, Red Hawk, were at once put to death.

This ended all hope of the treaty with the Shawnees, and while the regular Indian tribes, including the larger part of the Shawnees, join Branch and La Corne, the fragments of the Eastern tribes who had sought shelter in the West, and who were smarting under the many defeats which they had suffered at the hands of the white man, together with a part of the Shawnees, were organized as the Mingos (scattered or cast out) and sent in squads to annoy and destroy the settlements on the border.

The Indians thus operating in the Sandy and

Guyandotte Valleys were under the command of a white renegade, named Boling Baker, who was a noted horse thief—and cared more for horses than scalps—although when required to do so, he could brain a child or lift a scalp from a woman with as little compunction of conscience as any of his Indian comrades, although he preferred to keep in the background as much as possible.

The settlers along the New, the East and Clinch Rivers were frequently annoyed by marauding bands of these scattered tribes. Leaving their hunting grounds in the Guyandotte and Sandy Valleys, they would cross the mountains and like birds of prey, pounce down on the infant settlements, murder the women and children or take them captive and drive off their stock to their camps along the Guyandotte and Sandy Rivers, until they could take them for sale to strongholds beyond the Ohio. It was in following the Indians on their return home from one of these raids that the white man first invaded the solitudes of the hill country south of the Kanawha.

In the spring or early summer of 1777 a party of Indians pounced down on a settlement near the falls of New River and drove off about twenty horses. The attack was made just before nightfall, and before a squad of men could be mustered to follow them, darkness had made pursuit impossible.

As none of the settlers had been murdered or were

taken prisoner, it was evident that the raid was for the purpose of thieving, and that the number of Indians in the neighborhood was small. Captain Charles Hull, a brave pioneer, collected a body of twenty men at once and as soon as it was light enough started in pursuit.

On the afternoon of the third day, finding that he was gaining very little, if any, upon the retreating savages, and being at a point which must have been near the present side of Oceana, he found an old trail which crossed the mountain, and believing from the general direction of the stream which he had been following, that he could cross the mountain and reach the stream below by shorter route than that of following its meanders, he followed the old trail and crossed the mountain, where he found a creek running to the westward.

Among the men with Captain Hunn were John Cook, James Hines, Thomas Calfee, and two brothers, Thomas Huff and Peter Huff. After going about twelve miles down the creek and just before nightfall of the third day they were suddenly met by another body of Indians who fired upon them, killing Peter Huff, and not knowing the strength of Captain Hull's force, at once retreated down the creek.

Captain Hull, fearing an ambuscade in the darkness, at once went into camp. After burying Peter Huff, believing that the body of Indians who had fired upon him was not the same that he had been pursuing, and fearing that they were in considerable force in the neighborhood, thought it best to retrace his steps to the settlement on the New River.

This is believed to have been the first time that the white man had trod the soil of Logan County. It is certainly the first of any of which we have any tradition.

Raids were now frequently made, but as a rule one Indian, after getting as far down the Guyandotte Valley as the present Gilbert's Creek, crossed over to the Tug River Valley, and a sanguinary engagement was fought near the dividing ridge between the two rivers.

Baker had his camp on what is now known as Horsepen Creek, a fork of Gilbert's Creek, where his stolen horses were kept. Hickory trees were peeled, and by tying the bark from tree to tree, pens were formed in which the horses were securely kept.

The place was chosen so that a convenient line of retreat was always open. If enemies came down the creek the horses could be taken up the creek, and by crossing a very small hill, striking the Guyandotte River at the present site of the Logan Courthouse, or if thought necessary, he could, by crossing another small hill, have taken them down Pigeon Creek for about thirty miles, striking the Sandy River, or what is now known as the Tug Fork, at the present site of Naugatuck.

Among the noted Indian fighters who saved settlements from the tomahawk and scalping knife were James Breckenridge, John Breckenridge, George

Booth, George Berry, John Cook, Thomas Caine, William Dingess, Green Guyan, Joseph Gilbert, James Hensley, Peter Huff, Elias Harman, Mathias Harman, Samuel Lusk, James Morris, Edward McDonald, Ben Stewart, John Sheets, Abner Vance, Joseph Workman, Ben White, and James White, three of whom (Thomas Cline, Peter Huff and Joseph Gilbert) were killed, and whose names are perpetuated in the names of the creeks, upon which they fell and are buried. Many of the others entered and surveyed lands on the waters of the Guyandotte and Sandy, some moved to and died within the present limits of Logan County, while nearly all of them have descendants who are now citizens of the county.

As early as 1777 Henry Harman, a native of Prussia, with his sons, Henry, George and Mathias, and Absalom Lusk made a settlement in what is now known as Ab's Valley, in what is now Tazewell County. The place selected by them had formerly been occupied by Indian lodges, and a portion of the land was ready for cultivation.

They were soon joined in their new settlement by John Draper, James Moore, James Evans, Samuel Wiley and George Maxwell, with their families and, thus strengthened, they felt themselves in a manner secure from Indian raids, and their horses and cattle were allowed to run at large in the fertile valley.

For a while all went well. The crops were planted

and the wild game so abundant in the valley was hunted, and peace and plenty was promised. Indian eyes, however, watched them from the wooded ridge to the west, and on a bright morning in early summer of 1778, Mathias Harman and John Draper were out hunting about a mile from the settlement when, becoming separated, young Harman shot a deer and then commenced to reload his rifle.

Before he had finished he was seized from behind by a stalwart Indian, and on looking up he saw several other Indians within a few feet of him, and he gave up without a struggle. The whoop, which the Indians raised at his capture, notified Draper of the fact and he hurried to the settlement with the news.

Henry Harman and his sons, Henry and George, at once seized their arms, and with Draper, pursued rapidly after the Indians whom they overtook, on what is now known as Harman's Branch, in McDowell County. Harman and his companions at once opened fire on the Indians, and when the fight was over the young Harman was a free man, and five of the Indians were dead on the field while the others had saved themselves by flight.

None of the whites were hurt except Henry Harman Sr., who was covered with wounds, six arrowheads having broken off in his flesh, which were not extracted until he had been carried back to his home by the boys. Draper is said to have deserted during the fight, and on reaching the settlement had reported that Harman and all his sons were killed.

Revenge is one of the strongest characteristics of the Indian, as well as all other uncivilized races, and doubtless the Indians who escaped with their lives from the fight of Harman's dreamed of being revenged upon the little settlement of Ab's Valley; yet bided their time until the little settlement should again feel themselves secure from attack.

The crops for 1779 had been scarcely planted, and young Mathias Harman was busy raising a company of Rangers to join the patriots in the Carolinas, when in the early part of the spring a party of some thirty Indians dropped, as if from the clouds, upon the little settlement, capturing first James Moore, who had gone to the pasture to look after his horses, and with a savage whoop, bursting into the houses, murdering the Wiley, Moore and Maxwell families, and capturing George Maxwell and Jennie Wiley, the wife of Samuel Wiley, and daughter of James Evans.

The alarm was soon given, and Captain Mathias Harman, with about forty men of the company which he had been raising, was soon in the saddle and ready for pursuit. General Preston, who had about 100 men in his command, was also notified, and made a junction with Harman the next day at or near the present site of Welch.

With this force they pushed down the Tug River

to its junction with the Levisa, and then down the Big Sandy as rapidly as possible, keeping their scouts in advance of them, but they failed to overtake the Indians; in fact they lost all sign of their trail after passing the mouth of James Creek on Tug River.

When within about eight miles of the mouth of Big Sandy, at what is now the mouth of White's Creek, the scouts reported a large force of Indians, estimated at a thousand warriors, in front of them, and rapidly advancing up the river. The men had not stopped to hunt on the march, and they were entirely without provisions, and the forced march, which they had made, had jaded both horses and men.

Less than one hundred and fifty men in a wilderness, more than two hundred miles from a settlement, confronted by a wily and savage foe, numbering more than five to one, and acquainted with every mountain pass in the country by which a party could have been thrown in their front and an ambuscade formed, was indeed a critical position.

To fight was certain death and every retreat promised but little else. Nothing else, however, remained to be done, and posting his most experienced men in the rear of the column, General Preston and his brave men, chagrined at their failure in recapturing the pioneers who had been taken from Ab's Valley, set out upon their weary retreat up the river.

In the meantime a heavy rain had commenced, and

the mountain streams were in places overflowing their banks, making fording at times difficult, while the soft and yielding earth doubled the labor of the jaded steeds.

The weary march was kept up during the night, but without incident. The next morning both deer and buffalo were in sight, but they were afraid to fire a gun lest their Indian pursuers might locate them and hurry forward or worse still, send a column by some nearer route to intercept them.

Arriving at the mouth of Marrowbone they found the carcass of a buffalo which had been left by the Indians on their retreat down the river, and the bones, with what flesh had been left upon them, were divided among the men.

A short distance above Marrowbone they came upon a gas spring, which had been lighted. Here they paused for the purpose of resting their horses, and of roasting, as best they could, the meat and bones that they had found at the mouth of Marrowbone.

Some of the men, to satisfy their hunger, cut the tugs from their saddles and roasted them over the spring. After a short rest the gallant little band again took up their line of march up the river.

Arriving at the mouth of Pigeon, they found that Charles Lewis, who had been taken sick on their march down the river, and left at that place in charge of two companions, had died. They hastily dug a grave and buried him, but just as the last sad rites were being completed, scouts reported the Indian column but a short distance below.

Examining the creek, and finding it out of its banks and covered with driftwood and debris, they concluded that it was dangerous to attempt to cross it in the face of the foe, and leaving the old trail, they took up their line of march up the northeastern bank of the creek, hoping to find further up the stream where it could be forded a gap in the mountain by which they could return to the old trail of the river.

Arriving at what is now the mouth of Hell Creek, they went up that stream, thinking it would lead them to the old trail, but after proceeding about three miles they found in front of them an impassable barrier of stone, and they were forced to retrace their steps to Pigeon, expecting to encounter there the whole force of Indians.

Every gun was examined and a fresh charge of powder put in every pan of their flintlock rifles. On reaching Pigeon they were agreeably surprised in meeting their scouts to learn that the Indians had gone into camp at the mouth of the creek, throwing only a few scouts across the creek on the old trail.

General Preston then determined to follow the creek to its head, intending to rest for a while wherever game could be found. A short distance up the creek and at the mouth of a small creek flowing into Pigeon from the eastward, several elks were seen, which were speedily brought down by the trusty rifles, and the party went into camp, picketing their horses so they could feed on the wild grass which was abundant.

There were no signs of Indians during the afternoon or night, and after partaking of a hasty meal the next morning the command slowly resumed its march up the creek. A hunting party under the charge of Ben Cole was sent on in advance for the purpose of hunting game and fixing up a camp for the next night.

This little party pushed to the front, leaving a trail by which the main column could be guided, never leaving the creek until they came to its head. Here they crossed over the mountain and wended their way down a small stream until they came to what is now known as the "Forks of Ben Creek," where they found both game and grass abundant, and Cole selected it as the camping ground for the night and made preparations for the command, sending a part of his men out to kill game.

General Preston on arriving went into camp, and next morning, having heard nothing further of the Indian force, determined to give his men and horses a much-needed rest. Subsequently other scouts were sent out in every direction for the purpose of finding out what they could of the surrounding country, as well as their distance from the old trail over which they had traveled.

It was soon ascertained that they were within a mile of the old trail that led up the Tug River, and that they were really camped on another trail that led from the river up the creek. Scouts following this latter trail found it crossed over a gap of a mountain to another creek that flowed into the Guyandotte River, and now known as Gilbert's Creek.

After resting a few days General Preston sent the command of Captain Harman back to the settlements, and crossed with his command to the Guyandotte River, where, after reconnoitering the country as far down as the mouth of Buffalo Creek and then after resting a few days and feasting on the buffalo which were found in large herds, he took up his line of march for the settlements, passing up Huff's Creek by the grave of Peter Huff, which being recognized by some of the men who were with Huff when he was killed, the command paused and refilled the sunken grave with fresh earth and marched back to the settlements on the New River by the same route over which Captain Hull had returned two years before.

The beautiful valley of the Guyandotte, with its clear, running waters and its delightful climate, its generous soil and abundance of the finest game, was an inviting field for the white man, and many of the men who were with General Preston determined to possess it in spite of the lurking savage and countless dangers which they would have to encounter.

For this purpose parties were formed upon their arrival at the settlements. Their heroic struggle against want and privation, as well as against the red man, and of the brave manner in which they surmounted difficulty after difficulty, will partially be told in another chapter.

The information taken back to the settlements by Preston and Harman led to the speedy organization of parties, both in Montgomery and Washington, for the purpose of making further investigation and locating the lands in the rich valleys of the Guyandotte and Sandy for entry and survey.

As soon as the crops were gathered in the early autumn of 1779, and the supplies laid in for the comforts of families during the winter, two parties, well equipped with mountain rifles, powder and lead and such provisions and blankets as would be needed for the winter, set out across the mountain range that separated the settlements on the frontier from the almost unexplored wilderness, almost at the same time.

The venerable Absolom Lusk, an old Indian fighter, who was being cramped by civilization budding in Ab's Valley, which had taken its name from him, led the party from Washington, while the no less noted "Green" Guyan was in charge of the party from Montgomery.

The former party, after crossing the mountain, directed their steps down the waters of Sandy River, while the latter proceeded down the fertile valley of Guyandotte.

Scouts soon discovered that the country was

covered with large hunting parties of Indians, and the party under Absalom Lusk went into camp at the forks of the Tug, while the party of Green Guyan bivouacked at the mouth of Indian Creek, and the packhorses were sent back to the settlements.

Thrown thus into close proximity with each other and hunting on the same ground, there were almost daily skirmishes between the whites and Indians on Little Huff, Cub and Gilbert's Creek, of the Guyandotte, and War, Long Pole, Four Pole, and Turkey Creeks, of the Tug.

Thomas Caine had been killed in one of the encounters on Little Huff Creek, but he died game and his comrades had the proud satisfaction of knowing that he had assisted in sending scores of Indians to the happy hunting grounds.

CHAPTER VI

Whites Pursue Indians In Guyan Valley

Finding that the Indians were encamped with a strong force on Horsepen Fork of Gilbert's Creek and Ben Creek, and that the way was not then open for a further investigation of the Guyandotte and Tug Valleys, the hardy pioneers, after locating a few places for entry and survey in the new counties of Wyoming and McDowell, abandoned their camps and returned to the settlements, with the intention of again visiting the country as soon as the crops for the next season were planted.

Boling Baker, the renegade leader of the Indians, either emboldened by the withdrawal of the whites, or fearful lest it was his last opportunity to invade the settlements for pillage, set out as soon as the spring of 1780 opened up, for the frontier settlements along the waters of New River.

Leaving his men in the Flat Top mountain region, he went to the little settlement on the Bluestone and mixed freely with the people, telling them that he had been a captive, and had been with the Indians for several years, that in order to escape, he had assumed great admiration for them and had entered into their sports, that he had at last been admitted to tribal relations, and was fully trusted by them in everything.

He said he knew all of their strongholds, and every inch of ground in the Guyandotte Valley; that upon the opening up of spring the Indians who spent their winter in the Guyandotte Valley had returned to the country beyond the Ohio, and that the whole country was clear of Indians, and would remain so until they would come out again to hunt in the autumn.

In this manner he made the whites believe that they were entirely secure, and the vigils which had been kept over their stock and homes were relaxed. Baker made himself acquainted with everything in the settlement, and after a few days' sojourn among those whose sympathy he had aroused by the tale of his hardships and privations, he departed with the benediction of the good old dames, to join, as they supposed, his aged father and mother in the East, of whom he had spoken so lovingly, but really to join his Indian companions at the rendezvous in the mountains.

With knowledge thus gained, Baker only needed a favorable opportunity to execute his well-laid plans. With great caution they approached nearer and nearer to the little settlement, which they were able to do from the fact that it was the busy season, and there were no hunting parties abroad.

A dark, rainy night in the early part of April furnished the opportunity. A hard day's toil had prepared the pioneers for an enjoyment of "tired Nature's sweet restorer," and while they slept, dreaming, perchance, some of them, of days of childhood, and others, perchance, of the untaken land to the westward, which was inviting them to find homes, amid the shades of its unbroken wilderness. Baker and his men were busy in their work of securing their horses and preparing for flight.

On awakening the next morning and going out to feed the stock, each one of the settlers found that his horses were gone. Whether stolen or broken from their confinements on account of the storm, was not at once determined, but when search was made and neighbor met with neighbor, each with the same tale to tell, the truth flashed upon them that it was the work of Indians, and that the paleface stranger, who had discoursed so eloquently of the sufferings he had undergone in his captivity, was in some way connected with the thieving band.

That it was Indians was certain, and as no one had been killed, and no cabin burned, it was equally certain that none of the Indians were loitering in the neighborhood, but had rapidly fled with their booty.

Of the thirty horses in the settlement not one was

left, and it was ten miles to the next settlement and more than twenty miles to an organized mounted company. To follow mounted Indians, who had at least six hours start, on foot was foolishness. A messenger was at once sent to the next settlement to secure such horses and men as was possible and at the same time have some one take the news to the mounted guard of Montgomery.

The men of the settlement then divided; some to set everything about their homes in order, and prepare for the long journey, and the others to locate the trail over which the Indians had taken their horses.

John Breckenridge, a young man of great strength and determination, and who had been appointed as one of the deputies of William Ingles, the sheriff of the county, was found at the next settlement, and dispatched at once a courier to notify his chief of the raid.

He then addressed himself to the task of organizing the men of the settlement, and securing horses for those whose horses were stolen. Securing fifteen picked men and thirty-five horses, he set out for the raided settlement at about the middle of the afternoon, arriving there just before nightfall, where he found the men who had been sent out to locate the trail over which the stolen horses had been taken, possessed sufficient information to make the route certain.

He at once set the men and women to work to

prepare provisions for a ten days' journey, and to shell corn for the horses, as the young grass was not thought to afford sufficient nutriment for a hard march over a new country. During the night a courier arrived from Sheriff Ingles, notifying the little party that he would be with them as early as possible the next day, and to put in their time in organizing and making preparations for an arduous and dangerous journey.

During the early afternoon Sheriff Ingles, accompanied by General Preston, arrived with about sixty men well equipped for the journey, with rations for ten days and corn for their horses loaded on the pack horses.

Breckenridge in the meantime had selected fifteen of the men in the settlement to go with his party, and five of the stoutest horses were assigned to the duty of carrying the heavy packs, and Sheriff Ingles found everything in readiness for the journey upon his arrival.

A council of war was at once held, and General Preston, whose experience in public affairs made his opinion on all subjects law to the brave pioneers, after hearing the whole story of the paleface stranger and the consummate skill in taking the horses, came to the conclusion that the stranger was none other than Boling Baker, and that the horses would be kept for sometime at his rendezvous on the now Horsepen Fork of Gilbert, that there was no need of a hurried pursuit, but that the strength of both men and horses should be reserved until the enemy was sighted.

There was no dissent to his opinions, and while many of the hot blooded pioneers were no doubt anxious to set out upon the journey at once, upon his further advice the whole command went into camp at the settlement for the night.

The long and gloomy night was spent by the men in talking of the manner in which they desired their effects disposed of in the event they should never return, as well as in words of cheer and counsel of their loved ones, while Sheriff Ingles, Colonel Preston and the men whom they had gathered around for counsel, were maturing plans for their march upon the morrow.

It was finally agreed that neither Ingles or Preston would go with the party, which was put in command of William S. Madison, with John Breckenridge as second in command, while Green Guyan and John Carter were named as the trusted scouts. Guyan and Carter, in addition to the service which they had seen as scouts, were acquainted with the country as far as the mouth of Buffalo Creek, while their cool, determined bravery made them especially fitted for the service.

William Madison was a brother of Bishop Madison, of William and Mary College, and a son-in-law of Colonel Preston, and as a deputy surveyor under him had become inured to the privations of a life in the wilderness.

John Breckenridge was the son of Colonel Robert

Breckenridge and a brother of Alexander Breckenridge, the progenitor of the Breckenridge family of Kentucky. He was also the nephew of Colonel Preston, and as has already been said, the deputy of Sheriff Ingles. Although he had but reached his majority, he was the very impersonation of a soldier, not rash and impetuous as is so often the fault of youth, but was as cool and determined as men of mature years and experience in service.

The morning came, but the dark clouds which had hung over the Bluestone Valley since the night of the raid had not been lifted, and the drizzle of two days and nights had been succeeded by a downpour of rain; yet, notwithstanding the weather, everything was ready and every man in his place at the hour appointed for the march.

After tender embraces in every household, kisses were imprinted on the lips of loved ones as they were commended to the loving, watchful care of "Him who never slumbers," and hasty farewells were said.

Drawing their command in line in front of Preston and Ingles, the new commanders asked for such other words of instruction as they thought proper to give, and after receiving them the little party, now numbering about ninety men, marched with slow measure tread up the Bluestone Valley.

After going a few miles up the valley the party debouched to the right and were soon in the wilderness of the now far-famed Flat Top Mountain, and its summit was reached in time for the midday meal.

In the meantime the rain had ceased and the dark clouds of the morning had rolled to the eastward, and were hovering over the valley which they had just left, while to the west were mountains piled upon mountains as far as the eye could reach, whose irregular sides and summits, like the billows of the storm-tossed ocean, spoke of the grandeur and power of "Him who holds all things as if in the hollow of His hand."

The flowers of the wild cherry and maple and the blue violet and phlox, which were upon every side of them, represented the colors of their country's flag, while the bright April sun beckoned them to follow him westward, and at the same time seemed to speak to them of the omnipresence of Him, whom they trusted.

With these hardy pioneers Christianity was not a theory, but a fact. With implicit faith in the efficacy of the atonement of Christ, they loved him because he made it, and with full confidence in the truth of God, they entertained no doubt of His promises. Equally free from the Pharisaical cant of the covenantor and the empty formality of the churchman, they asked counsel of God, and determined to follow the guidance of His spirit as the dutiful child would follow the teachings of the devoted mother.

The meal being over, they once more committed themselves and their loved ones to God's care and mounted their horses for the journey. Turning slightly to the left they directed their course nearly southwest to the Guyandotte Mountains upon whose rugged crest they encamped for the night.

CHAPTER VII

Battling the Indians Far in the Wilderness

Next morning their course was along the crest of the mountain until, reaching the headwaters of Rock Castle Creek, they turned down the sides of the mountain along the stream and followed it to its mouth, thence down the main river to the mouth of the Clear Fork.

Heavy rains had been falling during the day, and the waters were rapidly rising, but finding that the Clear Fork could be forded, they crossed over and camped for the night on the west bank of the stream. The rain continued during the night, and the morning brought but little abatement.

The streams were swollen and in many places were overflowing the banks, and the little party was forced to abandon the valley, and make its way along the sides of the mountain. After a slow and weary march over rocks, precipices and tanglewood, the valley of the Gilbert was spied about the middle of the afternoon, and the party halted while Guyan and Carter were sent forward to reconnoiter and see if the Indians were still encamped at their old rendezvous on Horsepen.

A party of twelve men were detailed to go with Carter and Guyan to the river, taking axes with them for the purpose of constructing a raft to take the scouts across the river.

The scouts were ordered to cross the river about a mile above the mouth of Gilbert and proceed cautiously across the mountain to the mouth of Horsepen, and if no Indians were discovered, to wait until daylight, in order to examine and note carefully every sign about the camp, to ascertain when the camp had broken up, and in what direction the Indians were gone; but if Indians were discovered to return as quickly as possible and to fire no gun, unless it was absolutely necessary.

Ten of the men were ordered to remain at the place where the scouts had crossed, and the other ten were ordered to go down the river to a point opposite the mouth of Gilbert, where they could watch across the river for any sign of Indians, or perchance hear the report of rifles if the scouts were forced to fight.

The long hours of the night seemed to drag a weary length, and the gray dawn of the morning brought no report from the scouts. While this was evidence that the Indian camp had been abandoned, yet there was that unrest which uncertainty brings depicted in the face of all. It might be that the scouts, with all their caution, had been captured, and some of the men were anxious to cross the river to get some tiding of them.

As soon as it was sufficiently light Breckenridge was sent to join the little squad at the mouth of the creek, as that would be the place which the scouts would first report if the Indian camp had been abandoned.

He had but a little while to wait before the scouts appeared on the opposite side of the river and reported that the Indians had been gone for several days, and that their trail led up the creek to the westward. Madison was at once notified of the fact and after a short consultation it was decided to send two of the men across the river with provisions for the scouts, who were ordered to follow the trail up the creek and across the first mountain for the purpose of learning definitely the direction which the Indians had taken, but not to go so far as to prevent them from returning during the afternoon.

All of the men were then moved down to the bottom opposite the mouth of Gilbert and hunting parties were sent out to replenish their stock of provisions, while the horses were permitted to feed on the young grass.

Before the nightfall the scouts returned with the report that the trail had crossed over the mountain and had then turned down a creek, which creek they thought from its course flowed into the Guyandotte River. The trail indicated that there were from thirty to forty horses, and that about half of them were shod.

This convinced the men that it was the same band which they had been following, and they were eager to resume the pursuit, hoping to overtake them before they reached the Ohio. The river which had been very high for two days was still rising, which made it impossible to follow the trail, and council of war in which every one participated was held, and it was determined to move down the eastern bank of the river toward the Ohio.

With this course agreed upon, and placing their sentinels around the camp to prevent a surprise, the little band of Virginians, committing themselves and families to "Him who never sleeps," threw themselves upon the ground to rest until the coming of the morning.

The sound of the horn, as the first streaks of dawn had appeared in the east, awakened the weary slumberers from their dreams to the active duties of real life. Thanks were returned to the Giver of all good gifts for His protecting care and His fatherly protection, and guidance was asked for the day.

The horses were given grain and the morning meal hastily prepared, and where the sun had risen sufficiently to throw his ray direct on the narrow valley, the command was ready for its march down the river. A scouting party of ten picked men, including Guyan and Carter, were placed under the command of Breckenridge and thrown to the front, while the remainder of the command, with Madison in front, followed at convenient distance.

The march for the first six miles was very slow and difficult. The foaming waters of the swollen river dashed their waves against the rocky sides of the mountains, forcing the men to go up the steeps where ever and anon they encountered cliffs which were impassable. Onward, however, was the watchword as obstacle after obstacle was encountered and overcome, with the determination which is born of the blending of Puritan and Cavalier.

Six miles below the mouth of Gilbert a bottom was reached at the mouth of a small creek and the marching became easier. A mile still lower down another creek was reached and a herd of elk found grazing on its banks.

As quick as thought the stillness was broken by the report of several rifles and two of the elks were brought to the ground, and were taken and cleaned before the main party, under Madison, come up, having hastened forward at the report of rifles, fearing that the advance party had been attacked by Indians.

The party were soon in the saddle again and at noon they halted at the mouth of Buffalo, now the present site of Man, for the midday repast, and here the horses were again permitted to feed on the young grass.

After a short rest the command was once more ready for the march. On the north bank of the creek there was a steep, rocky bluff, some thirty or more feet in height, which, together with the back water from the river, barred the way, and the command went up the creek about a half mile, where it was easily forded and the first bench on the mountain reached without difficulty.

They were now in a country which was entirely new to them, and upon which probably the foot of no white man with the probable exception of Boling Baker, or some captive who had never returned, had been set. The river and an old and almost indistinct trail were their only guides.

Over this trail they pushed, sometimes in the broad sandy bottoms, then through deep ravines which had been created by waters which for centuries poured down from the mountains, then over knolls which jutted to the vary margin of the river, or rocky precipices which seemed to be suspended immediately over the yawning waters which foamed and dashed their angry waves against the base of the mountain.

Eight miles below Buffalo a large creek (Rum Creek) was crossed and three miles on another creek, (Dingess Run) was reached. Here fresh Indian signs were plainly visible and the command halted.

Guyan and Carter were sent down the river and two other scouts were sent up the creek. The scouts that were sent up the creek soon returned and reported that the freshest signs all pointed down the creek, and that there were no Indians above.

Just before nightfall Guyan and Carter returned and reported that about two miles below they had discovered on a large island ten Indian lodges, and that there were a large force of Indians with horses and cattle, but as the island was thickly covered with a growth of cane it was impossible to accurately estimate their number, that the high water would make it impossible for them to attack the Indians, and that they were certain from the quiet manner of the Indians that they were not aware of the presence of any whites in the neighborhood.

After consultation it was thought best to go into camp in the bottom on the south bank of the creek; so, after partaking of their evening meal, securing their horses, and throwing a strong guard around the camp, and sending ten picked men a few hundred yards below the mouth of the creek, the men lay down to sleep, their rifles within easy reach.

Everything was quiet during the night and the weary watchers had nothing to report when they were relieved by those who had rested during the night.

As soon as it was light enough, Breckenridge, with the two scouts, Guyan and Carter, ascended halfway up the high mountain situated a short distance below the mouth of the creek, in order to locate the Indian lodges and their surroundings. The heavy fog, however, which hung over the river as a dark pall, hid the island and all the surrounding valley from their view.

The scene before them, however, was grand. A landscape which the brush of the painter cannot convey was spread out before their eyes. Mountain piled upon mountain, while huge rocks like mighty giants crowned their summits, and the fog-covered valley seemed to be guarded on every side by petrified sentinels.

Slowly the sun lifted himself above the wood crests of the mountains, and the greatest of all painters threw over the scene His own lights, melting and rolling away the mist, and revealing to the eye a valley more lovely than that of the far-famed Glenvaliah.

A large creek whose banks were lined with green grass and flowering shrubbery and over whose course huge trees reached their limbs as if to shelter it from the light of the day, flowed from the west, and dividing its waters when almost within a stone's throw of the river, emptied itself into the river at two points nearly half a mile apart, forming a lovely island, which was covered with a luxuriant growth of cane, and upon which, near the southwestern point, were ten Indian lodges, around which were seen several groups of Indians, while near the center of the island were some forty horses and a few cattle leisurely grazing.

Enchanted with the scene, young Breckenridge feasted his eyes for some time upon its grandeur and seemed oblivious of everything else until Guyan reminded him that there were arduous and pressing duties before them. He at once closed his glass and returned to camp at the mouth of the creek, when everything that he had seen was fully reported and discussed.

It was at last determined that rafts should be constructed, and that Breckenridge should cross the river with half the command and approach as near as possible to the island, when he should rest until night, and then cross the upper arm of the creek and make a dash on the lodges and capture the horses and kill as many Indians as possible.

Madison was to leave his camp just before nightfall and secure a position near the lower mouth of the creek, and as the firing commenced on the upper part of the island he was to open fire on the lower part in order to create as great confusion as possible among the Indians.

The rafts were at once constructed and Breckenridge, with forty-five men, crossed the river and went up the wooded side of the mountain so as to be protected from view. About the middle of the afternoon, when he had reached a position on the ridge which overlooked the whole of the island, he discovered the Indians were in an excited manner crossing the river at the lower end of the island.

It was then apparent that the Indians had in some way learned that the whites were on the opposite side of the river and that their crossing the river was for the purpose of making a night attack on the whites.

Breckenridge at once sent a messenger to notify Madison of his danger and to advise him to march to the attack while it was still daylight, and that as soon as the first gun was fired he would attack the lodges and secure the horses.

Madison at once put the lead horses in charge of some men who were instructed to follow the command a short distance behind, and with the other forty men he moved swiftly to attack.

The Indians, though taken by surprise, fought like devils, until the firing on the island commenced, when they broke and fled for their canoes which were tied to the lower end of the island.

Not a white man was killed, and only two slightly wounded, while six of the Indians were killed, and some ten or twelve wounded, all of whom were captured, and among the latter was a woman of some forty or sixty years of age, who from her dress and brave bearing was at once recognized as the leader of the party. With the exception of the woman, the wounded Indians were quickly disposed of, no one caring to be bothered with a captive Indian.

Breckenridge had but slight opposition on the island, and succeeded in capturing fifty horses, a few cows and about fifty bushels of corn and killing three Indians, and that without the loss of a single man. About twenty Indians with their horses made their escape from the island when the attack was first made. So ended what is known as the "Battle of the Islands."

Approaching darkness made pursuit dangerous, and the men lay upon their arms during the night.

With the return of morning a consultation was made between Madison and Breckenridge, and it was agreed to gather whatever could be carried from the island, burn the rest of the lodges, then throw the commands together and get ready to march home, as further pursuit of the Indians would be useless.

Breckenridge at once set to work, in gathering the skins from the lodges which he, with corn, horses and cattle moved over to the camp of Madison, and then burned the lodges, bringing all of his command over long before nightfall. In the meantime Madison and his men had buried the body of Aracoma according to her request. The afternoon was spent in making such notes of the country as would be useful to them in the future, and early the next morning the command set out on its return to the settlement which was reached without incident on the fourth day.

The spring had well advanced when the hardy mountaineers had reached their homes, and they at once set to work to make up the lost time in preparing the soil for the planting of the year's crop, expecting to again visit the valley of the Guyandotte in the latter part of the summer or the early autumn.

CHAPTER VIII

America Gains Her Independence

The planting of the crops was, however, scarcely finished before they heard of the capture of Charleston, South Carolina, by the British, and the surrender of the Patriot army by General Lincoln, to Clinton, on the 11th day of May. This startling news was soon followed by that of the massacre of four hundred Virginians and Carolinians, the command of Colonel Abraham Buford, by the cavalry of Tarleton, on the Waxhaw, which took place on the 29th of the same month.

The Carolinians were prostrate and helpless at the feet of the well-equipped forces of Cornwallis, Cruger and Brown, while the Tories, emboldened by British success, were scouring the country, marking their course with the blackened ruins of once happy homes, driving women and children to the wilderness for shelter, sending the men to Charleston as prisoners, enforcing them to join in the destruction of the property of those who were known to have espoused the cause of the Patriots. To so great an extent had this been done that Clinton wrote to Germain, "There are but few men in South Carolina who are not our prisoners or in arms with us."

The troops with which Washington intended to aid Lincoln were still in Virginia under DeKalb, and Governor Jefferson was doing all he could to fill up its ranks with fresh levies from the country east of the Blue Ridge. Congress put Gates in command of the army thus raised, who hurried forward, striking the well-drilled legions of Cornwallis at Sanders Creek, only to be hurled back, bleeding and dismayed, to Charlotte.

In the meantime Governor Jefferson gave to Robert Campbell, who had already won renown as an Indian fighter on the border, a Colonel's commission, and authorized him to raise a regiment of mounted riflemen to be attached to the brigade of General William Campbell, of Augusta County. Montgomery County was called on to furnish two hundred men for this regiment, and although she had given nearly a thousand of her sons to the Patriot Army, she responded at once and her fresh levies were soon ready for the field.

Soon after the defeat of Gates at Sander Creek, the command of Sumpter had been nearly annihilated at Fishing Creek by the cavalry of Tarleton. Major Patrick Ferguson had in the meantime been sent with eight hundred regular cavalry to gather and enlist the Tories in the mountains to the west of Broad River, and everything seemed to be growing more gloomy for the Patriots.

About the first of October the command of General Campbell, consisting of the skeleton regiments of Campbell, Cleveland, McDonald, Sevier, Shelby and Williams, were camped near the present town of Spartanburg, South Carolina.

Learning that Ferguson was at King's Mountain with his regulars and a body of Tories, Campbell selected nine hundred of his mounted riflemen, and on the night of the 6th set out to attack him. The march was continued during the night, and on the afternoon of the next day they came near Ferguson's camp.

Dismounting, they advanced in four columns. The regiments of Shelby and Campbell, which formed the center, marched first up the hill and brought on the attack, and for a few minutes it seemed as if the bayonets of the regulars were superior to the clubbed rifles of the mountaineers, but Sevier and Williams on the right and Cleveland and McDonald on the left, falling upon the now surprised Ferguson, drove his command into a hollow where Ferguson was killed and DePeyster, of the King's American regiment, surrendered the command.

The loss of the British was over eleven hundred men and fifteen hundred stand of arms, while the mountaineers lost only twenty-eight killed, and sixty wounded.

Thus it will seem that the same men that broke up the last settlement of the Indians on the Guyandotte, in the same year, assisted in crowning the crest of King's Mountain with a halo of glory which will never fade so long as the English language is spoken or men love to recount the heroic deeds of brave men in their struggles for liberty.

The victory at King's Mountain was the first rift in the clouds that hung over the Patriots of the Carolinas, and gave them fresh courage while at the same time it staggered the royal power, forced Cornwallis to draw in his bands of marauders and concentrate his forces, and retreat from his advance position in North Carolina to the strongholds of Ninety-Six and Camden, in which retreat he was annoyed almost at every step by bands of Whigs, who had taken fresh courage from the defeat of Ferguson.

The Patriots were rising everywhere, and Marion and Sumpter were every day annoying the British outposts. On the 30th of October, General Nathaniel Green was appointed to succeed Gates in the command of the Southern army, and the command of Campbell was at once attached to his command and remained with him until the 14th day of December, 1782, when Charleston was finally evacuated by the British and turned over the the civil authorities of South Carolina.

While with Green our mountaineers covered themselves with glory at Cowpens, Guilford Court House,

Hobkirk's Hill, Ninety-Six, Eutaw Springs and the many minor engagements which are not known to history.

Many of these who served with Campbell, both from Montgomery and Washington, entered and surveyed land in Logan County. Some of them settled here in person, and spent their declining years in our salubrious climate and many of our best citizens are descended from them and from their brethren whose graves are kept green in the highlands of the Old Dominion.

CHAPTER IX

Surveying Parties Enter Guyandotte Valley

There were a few surveying and hunting parties sent out from Montgomery County to the Guyandotte and Cole River Valleys during the years of 1781, 1782, and 1783, but with the exception of the making of a few surveys, some of which will be hereafter named, and a few skirmishes with the Indians, in one of which James Crawley was killed on the creek which bears his name, and in another Richard Hewett was killed on Cole River near the mouth of the creek which perpetuates his name, there was but little done in opening the country up for settlement.

The distance from the frontier settlements and the long stretch of wilderness which intervened, among whose shades were always prowling bands of Indians, had made the surveying both expensive and dangerous, and the planting and seating of the lands surveyed, as required by law, almost an impossibility.

Added to this was the heavy debt Virginia had

assumed in paying the expenses of the War of the Revolution, the burden of which caused many people of southwestern Virginia to join the people of western North Carolina in seeking to establish an independent State to be known as Frankland, and when Virginia, in 1786, gave a partial separate government to Kentucky and released its people from this tax, many of the people who were getting ready to settle up the Guyandotte Valley, went to Kentucky, and when, in 1787, the northwestern territory which had been ceded to Virginia by the general Government, was opened up to settlement by treaties made with the Indians, the tide of emigration went in that direction, and the occupancy of the Guyandotte and Sandy Valley was again postponed.

From 1780 to 1791, we have no account of any Indian raid on the border settlements of Montgomery and Washington. While the Indians surely roamed and hunted at will in the valleys of the Guyandotte, Sandy and Cole, they never ventured across the mountains that separated these valleys from the settlements of the whites, and the skirmishes that took place between them and the hunting and surveying parties seemed to be more accidental then premeditated—and the whites, as a rule, would have the advantage.

In violation of the treaty of 1783, the British still held many of the western posts. English avarice as usual was jealous of the American trader. Sir John Johnson, who had been the English Indian Agent in the Mohawk Valley, and Sir Guy Carleton, Governor of Canada, were through their agents fostering discontent among the Indians, and really inciting them to massacre the white settlers. The discontent had become so great that open hostilities were developed in the spring of 1790 and all attempts to quiet the Indians by peaceable arrangements were fruitless.

In September, 1790, General Harmon was sent out from Fort Washington (now Cincinnati) with about four hundred regulars and eight hundred volunteers to the headwaters of the Maumee to subdue the Indian revolt, but was himself defeated and forced to return. During the year Generals Scott and Wilkinson were sent to subdue them, and succeeded in burning many of their villages.

This, however, only tended to exasperate the Indians, and all of their old time enmity against the whites was aroused. Emissaries were at once sent among the Indians who were still roaming in bands in the mountains of western Virginia and Kentucky, and the spring of 1792 witnessed the donning of the war paint and the massing of the small bands into the larger ones.

Hunting parties in the Guyandotte, Cole and Sandy Valleys marked this strange conduct of the Indians, and the settlements were at once placed in a state of defense. Mounted riflemen were organized, whose duty it was to parole the mountains west of the settlements, while a mounted courier was kept at every settlement in order to make known to this organization any attack which might be made upon any of the settlements by any band of Indians which might escape their vigilant watch.

Henry Farley was placed in command of the company that guarded the settlements on lower Bluestone and with him were several others who will be mentioned among the early settlers of Logan County. Farley had seen service in the Carolinas with Colonel Campbell and was distinguished for his coolness and bravery.

About the middle of June while resting with his command near the head of Bluestone Creek, a scout came in with the report that a body of some two hundred Indians were cautiously advancing through the wilderness from the west. Captain Farley at once notified the nearest settlement of the fact and, sending his horses down the creek, formed his men so as to be sure to ambush the advancing savages.

Farley had but a little while to wait. The Indians were proceeding slowly in single file, almost unconscious of danger, when the Virginia yell and the sharp, deadly crack of the rifles threw them into consternation and scattered them in almost every direction. While Farley had only about fifty men with him, he ordered his horses to follow him, and pursued the Indians on foot, until night, when he halted on account of the darkness.

His horses coming up during the night, he pushed forward and overtook the savages in the afternoon on the headwaters of Cole River, when there was a running fight for several hours, darkness again putting an end to the conflict. The Indian trail was followed the next day down the river across the mountains to the waters of Little Cole, but nothing was seen of the Indians and the whites again camped for the night.

The next day Captain Farley's command followed the trail down Little Coal and across the mountain to the Guyandotte River and overtook the Indians about two miles below the present site of the Logan Court House, where three Indians were killed. Darkness again saved the redskins, and nothing more was seen of them until the Falls of Guyandotte were reached just before nightfall the next day, when a squad of seven were killed.

The next morning Farley went as far as the mouth of the river, but nothing more was seen of the Indians, and he returned home. Among the men who were with Captain Farley was William Dingess, who will hereafter be more prominently mentioned. At the Falls of Guyandotte he cut the skin from the forearm of an Indian and made a razor strop of it which he kept until his death.

A party of Indians belonging to this band, leaving the main command, while within the present limits of Raleigh County, came upon a hunter's hut which was built by four of the Clay brothers. Only one of the brothers was found in the hut, and he was at once killed and scalped.

The other brothers, coming from hunting a short time afterwards, found the dead body of their brother, and following the Indians to the present site of Boone Courthouse, killed two of the them, the others escaping.

We have but one other raid to record, which we take from "Bickley's History of Tazewell County." In the latter part of the summer of 1792, Major Robert Crockett, of Wythe County, was informed that a considerable band of Indians had been seen in the settlement of the Clinch, endeavoring to steal horses, but had not at that time succeeded.

He immediately raised a company of forty and went in pursuit of them, thinking it likely that he should fall in with them as they were leaving the settlement with their booty. He found the trail over which they had passed but a short time since, and having no doubt of the route they would take, concluded that it would be an easy matter to come up with them at night. Being short of provisions, he stopped and ordered his men to separate in pairs and try to kill a few deer. They were to hunt but two hours when the march was to be resumed.

Joseph Gilbert and Samuel Lusk, acting as spies, were ordered to keep on and note carefully every sign, and, in case they found the Indians, to return and give information. These two men were noted spies, and had often served together. They continued on the trail for about an hour, where they came upon a lick, at which the Indians, who were also in need of provisions, lay concealed, waiting for the deer or elk which frequent it.

The Indians fired, missing Gilbert but wounding Lusk in the hand. Gilbert turned to run, and had made off a few yards when Lusk called to him to return and save him, if possible. The affectionate tone in which this appeal was uttered fired the manly heart of Gilbert, who turned about and shot the nearest Indian, who fell upon the spot.

The Indians closed in upon him as he stood over the body of Lusk, who had fainted from the loss of blood, but dropping his gun, he drew his heavy hunting knife and fell to work upon the naked bodies of his enemies with such spirit that the Indians no longer dared to approach within reach of his arm. Keeping out of his reach they began to hurl their tomahawks at him with such force and accuracy that he soon lay dead on the earth by the side of his now revived companion.

The wounded hand of Lusk was immediately cared for by the Indians, who, after scalping Gilbert, commenced a rapid march to the Ohio. The firing was too far off to give Major Crockett any warning of what was going on, but when the two hours had expired he took up the line of march and followed on after the two spies.

When they arrived at the lick they found the body of Gilbert, and pushed on with all possible speed, after burying him near the bank of the creek which now bears his name, but could not come up with the Indians.

The Indians told Lusk, whom they took prisoner, and who returned in a short time, that if Major Crockett had not stopped to hunt he must have cut them to pieces, as they were but a few moments before they came to the lick, engaged in catching young otters, their arms in the meantime lying on a knoll several rods from them.

Tradition tells us that Gilbert, after firing the shot which killed the Indian and realizing the hopelessness of his escape, bent his gun by striking it on a tree, in order to prevent it from falling into the hands of the Indians to be used by them against the pursuing whites, and the spot where he fell was marked by Major Crockett, and the branch, at whose mouth the tragedy was enacted, is still known as the "Twisted Gun."

No hostile Indian is believed to have ever put foot on Logan soil afterwards. Negotiations for peace were already being made between the United States and the Indian tribes of the Northwestern Territory, and the Indians in western Virginia returned to their strongholds west of the Ohio to wait the results of the negotiations.

The negotiations failed, but in the meantime

General Wayne, who had been placed in command of the western army, had massed a sufficient force to destroy the power of the savages and prevent them from making any further raids upon the settlements east of the Ohio. On the 20th of August, 1794, the battle of "The Fallen Timber" was fought, and the Indian power was forever broken.

After the burial of Gilbert, Captain Crockett pursued the Indians as fast as the circumstances would permit. The death of Gilbert and the capture of Lusk was a great loss to the little party, as there was no one with Crockett who could take their place. Gilbert had been for a long time an Indian scout, and was familiar, not only with the signs made by the Indians, but with every foot of the country.

Losing all signs of the Indians, Crockett, on reaching the present site of the town of Logan, gave up pursuit and went into camp, and started on his return to the settlements on the next day. Lusk was kept a prisoner for several years and upon his return stated that the Indians camped on the same night on what is now known as the "Backbone," and within less than a mile of the camp of Captain Crockett.

Lusk also stated that an Indian with a tomahawk in his hand stood over him during the night to prevent him from making a noise, and that as soon as it was light the next morning they crossed the mountain over to the waters of Hart's Creek and went down it to the

Guyandotte River, and then down the Guyandotte River to the Ohio, over which they had crossed in canoes.

Lusk lived for several years after his return, and many who are now living learned the story of his capture and captivity from his own lips. After one hundred and eighty-five years of fierce and savage warfare, in which neither age nor sex was spared, the soil of Virginia was the undisputed property of the aggressive Anglo-Saxon.

The conflict begun between the two races on Cape Henry, on the 1st day of May, 1607, was ended, the last hostile camps, where the two races lay upon their arms in sight of the present site of Logan, being broken up on a bright October morning, 1792, the Indians making their final retreat and taking with them their last Virginia prisoner.

These years had been rich in events. The little colony of one hundred and five Englishmen planted at Jamestown, on the 13th day of May, 1607, was now a mighty State of more than 700,000 souls. The ninety "agreeable young women, poor but respectable, and incorrupt," sent over by Sir Edwyn Sandys, in 1619, were the mothers of a great people. And the first representative government established in the New World, at Jamestown, on the 30th day of July, 1619, had now grown into fifteen free and sovereign states, united by a written constitution, in one general representative government, with Virginia's own beloved son as its

Chief Executive.

The citizens of Montgomery County now numbered about 14,000 inhabitants, and of Washington County about 6,000 inhabitants; Greenbrier, which had been cut off from Montgomery, 6,500 inhabitants, and Russel, which had been cut off from Washington, 3,500 inhabitants, a total of 30,000 inhabitants, all of whom had fully discharged their duties in the trying ordeal.

Descended from the men who had met and triumphed over the Confederacy of Powhatan, the Nottoways, the Meherrins, and other of the Algonquin tribes east of the Blue Ridge, they had taken up the work where their fathers had left it, and had succeeded not only in driving the last of the mighty Shawnees, the most warlike of the Algonquin tribes, from Virginia, but had contributed their part in the establishment of free governments for the American States.

When in 1710, Spotswood, with his company of horsemen, ascended one of the highest points of the Appalachian ranges and gazed upon the mountains and valleys to the westward, the most sanguine of the party did not dream of its being the center of the greatest civilized power in the world.

The men, however, who accepted from him the golden horseshoe with the inscription, "Sic Jurat transcendere Montes" (thus he swears to cross the mountain), were obedient to the requirements of the "Order of the Knights of the Golden Horseshoe," and set to work at once to conquer the country and, dying while in the line of duty, left to their descendants the completion of work so bravely begun.

In the later part of 1755, or the early part of 1756, there was an attack made by the Indians all along the border, and a regiment composed of sixteen companies was raised east of the Blue Ridge and placed under the command of Washington for defense, and the General Assembly of Virginia, in 1756, ordered the building of a line of forts along the border from the Potomac to the North Carolina line. The next year (1757) Governor Dinwiddie sent Major Andrew Lewis with a force of 410 men, 263 of these being whites and 147 Cherokee Indians, for the purpose of destroying the Indian villages on the Ohio River.

Among the officers in this expedition were Archibald Alexander, Henry Guyan, Peter Hogg, John Montgomery, James Overton, William Preston, Richard Pearis, David Stewart, John Smith and Obidiah Woodson, Richard Pearis being in charge of the Cherokee Indians.

This is known as the "Sandy Creek Expedition," and it is believed that it went as far as the forks of Sandy, where the command established a camp and remained until it was recalled by John Blair, the President of the Council, who was acting as Governor. The expedition accomplished nothing, and the route over which it marched is not known.

The settlers on the frontier found in the Shawnee Indian, with whom they first came in contact on the Roanoke, a more wily foe than any with whom they had to deal east of the Blue Ridge. While the Algonquin family it is though that they came eastward about the middle of the seventeenth century, and occupied the valley along the Ohio River and its tributaries from the waters of the Tennessee, on the south, to the mouth of the Muskingum on the north, the Cherokees joining them on the south, and the great Iroquois confederacy on the north.

In 1760 the Shawnees were said to have numbered at least 75,000 souls, with some 15,000 braves, always ready for the warpath, and in addition to their wars with the whites, they were always in trouble with their neighbors on the north and south, and were at times in subjection to the Iroquois, who claimed a kind of sovereignty over them.

While there were some great men in the Shawnee tribe, among them were Cornstalk and Tecumseh, the greatest of the Indian sachems, yet as a rule the animal propensities strongly predominated over the intellectual. The Shawnee Indian is described as of haughty demeanor, taciturn and stoical to the highest degree, yet revengeful in the destruction of his enemies, cruel to his prisoners without regard to age, sex or condition, but enduring captivity and even the most painful tortures without a murmur.

Their diet consisted of parched corn and the flesh of the wild game or of the fish, so abundant in all of the tributaries of the Ohio. Their only drink was cold water, and their simple diet and drink, added to their training in long fasts and rigorous tortures, gave them a power of endurance which was not found in any other tribe.

Yet with all of their power they have fallen before the march of civilization, and in the census of 1890, one hundred years after their expulsion from Virginia, less than one hundred are reported surviving.

The Shawnees recognized a Supreme Being, and a host of spirits, good and evil, and believed in the future state of existence. They were very careful of their dead, collecting their remains and burying them in moss-lined graves with wreaths around their heads, and placing in the graves with them food and implements used in the chase.

The heads of the dead were placed to the east, in order that they might look to the west, whence they came, and where they expected to return to find the Happy Hunting Ground. Their burying grounds were selected on high ground above running water and a ditch was dug about a foot deeper than the graves, in order to carry off the water and prevent it from rising over their dead.

Of Boling Baker, the white leader of the scattered tribes, there is but little known. Many old men have seen on beech trees in this county, the following words carved: "Boling Baker, his hand and knife—He can't find a horse to save his life."